Damn
FEAR

Traneisha Y. Jones

Copyright © 2022 by Traneisha Y. Jones

All rights reserved. Printed in the United States of America. No part of this book may be used or reproduced in any manner whatsoever without written permission except in the case of brief quotations embodied in critical articles or reviews.

For information contact: www.damnfear.com

First Edition: May 2022

10 9 8 7 6 5 4 3 2 1

*For those who dare to dream,
and stumble on the way.*

TABLE OF CONTENTS

Foreword..i

Preface..iv

Introduction..1

The Root of Fear.......................................4

Good Things Fall Apart............................20

The Convenience of Settling.....................28

Stir Up the Gift.......................................33

The Voices of Fear..................................37

Name Your Fear......................................44

Defeating the Giant of Fear......................48

Scriptures for Overcoming Fear................51

Afterword..53

Questions for Reflection..........................56

Recommended Reading..........................58

ACKNOWLEDGMENTS

I am extremely grateful to everyone who made this book possible.

To my parents, Montrail and Demetris Tony, I am eternally grateful for your love and support. Thank you for teaching us to, "go out and get it." I love you.

To my Momo, Tracey Robinson. Thank you for the gift of you. You have a unique way of getting people together. I love you.

To Carolyn Husband, one of my biggest cheerleaders and agitators (lol), I appreciate you and love you dearly.

To Candace Jozef Semien, thank you for your support, guidance and accountability. You are truly a birther.

Foreword

I love the boldness Traneisha stepped into in writing this new book, *Damn Fear*. It literally takes someone to say, "Enough is enough! It's time to take my life back." It is amazing to see how many people never fully materialize their dreams, businesses, family and personal goals because of fear. Mostly because fear is a paralyzing agent that stops so many people in their tracks with so much unfulfilled potential.

If you think about it, for many people the determining factor between success and failure is fear's influence throughout their journey. It is whether or not you will allow your fears to get the best of you. Unfortunately, for many this has been the case; and the only accomplishment and inheritance that is left behind is regret.

Thank God for this new addition to the topic of fear and how to overcome it. I love the way Traneisha places herself within the pages of this book and becomes vulnerable to the readers. It is her vulnerability that gives her authority to speak on this topic.

Throughout this book you will masterfully discover many of the characteristics of fear and how they try to influence your life. You will also be given practical principles, wisdom, and encouragement in knowing how to identify these characteristics in your life and how to overcome them.

1 John 4:18 says, *"There is no fear in love; but perfect love casts out fear, because fear involves torment."* What this reveals is how fear wars against the finished work of Christ. Fear involves torment and Jesus did not die for you to live in torment. This is why fear has to be removed from your life.

You cannot afford to go another day with the same tormenting trepidation that has crippled you up to this point; and you cannot afford to go on without addressing what has been tormenting you. There may even be some of you who have found yourself defending your fears. Well, let me let you in on something. As long as you defend your fears they have the right to build a home in your life, but the moment you challenge them they lose their power and right to influence and dominate you.

It is important for you to understand that there isn't any type of fear that is ok. 2 Timothy 1:7 says that God has not given us a spirit of fear. In this verse, fear is identified as a spirit. In other words, all fear is spiritual. Whether it is a fear of demons, pain, darkness, purpose, failure, flying, people, or any other type of fear, you cannot afford to be comfortable with it in your life.

If we ever want to experience all God has for us we have to be willing to confront the fears that paralyze and cause us to doubt God and doubt ourselves. All fear is spiritual and none of it comes from God. My prayer is that as you take this journey through the pages of *Damn Fear*, that fear will truly be damned in your life and a new journey into hope, boldness, and confidence will begin!

Isaac Watson
Founder of Encounter Worship Center
Founder of Isaac Watson Ministries Inc.
Author of *Access Granted*, *Misplaced*, and other titles.
www.isaacwatsonministries.com

PREFACE

THAT DAMN FEAR has dethroned God.
He's in the driver's seat and I'm on the
Passenger side telling him to go right,
When God says go left.
"But there's a pot hole," I say.
Giving excuses, reasons for my disobedience
To God,
Devaluing myself
And the gift He's placed within Me.
SELFISH disregard for my purpose.
The WAY I SEE MYSELF and my
CIRCUMSTANCES has OVERSHADOWED the
WAY GOD SEES ME.
I've dug a grave for the VERY IDENTITY
I found in Christ.
And Graced it with a HEADSTONE that reads,
"I can't because…"
After all I have an obligation to fear,
Why? I don't know.
Some kinda way it comforts me.
I'm all SCREWED UP.
The very thing that HAUNTS ME
Also brings me comfort.
"DELIVER ME!" I cry.
Yet I find myself in the same place,
Still Standing

Standing Still
How can all of the faith, and none of the faith
Be housed in the same place?
That DAMN FEAR
Keeps driving me and
It's really quite sad, especially when I think of all I could have.
It's keeping me from my destiny and purpose.
I hope I can overcome it before it gets worse.
THAT DAMN FEAR has my vision all distorted,
Blurry visualizations,
Not seeing GOD AS-HE-REALLY-IS
A heart overcome by burdens,
Mind filled with doubt.
A mouth laced with DREAM OPPOSITION,
Robbing me of my RIGHTFUL POSITION.
That DAMN FEAR, DAMN, FEAR, D@M# FEAR!
CONDEMN Fear.
For those who God knew he also pre-ordained.

INTRODUCTION

"All are slaves to hope or fear."
- Seneca

I count it not strange that the moment I set out to write this book, I was met with fear. I literally write and edit books for a living, yet I found myself paralyzed and overwhelmed, unsure of what to say or how to say it. Actually, it wasn't that I didn't know what to say, it's that I second guessed everything that came to mind, "Was this the message people really needed to hear? Was what I saying good enough? Do I need to say more? Was it strong enough to compel people and inspire them to push past their own fears?" I literally coach people through this process, yet I found myself up against the same wall.

Fear is indiscriminate. It likes to settle on us and weigh us down. It keeps us stagnant, immobile, and running in circles. If we're not careful, fear can have us looking like the children of Israel,

Damn Fear

longing for the Promised Land, yet doing everything to sabotage our entry.

The vision for *Damn Fear* was birthed out of my own struggles and a desire to see others set free from the spirit of fear. It's my sincere hope that what I write will not only free me, but that you too would experience freedom in your own life.

I'm convinced that more than anything else, the spirit of fear is what keeps many of us from fully walking in God's purpose and plans for our lives. It's what keeps us in mediocrity, when God has called us to so much more.

As you read *Damn Fear*, I challenge you to strip yourself of fear and take up the mantle God has given you.

God has so much more in store for us, but in order to obtain those things we must get to the other side of fear. I hear you asking, "How?" Samuel Butler, a noted English author once said, "Fear is static that prevents me from hearing myself," but I would wager that fear is static that prevents us from hearing God. The question is, "Are we ready to listen?"

"When I am afraid,
I put my trust in you."

— *Psalm 56:3*

Chapter One
The Root of Fear

"Free your mind and the rest will follow."
- EnVogue

What is the root cause of fear? Maybe if we knew the answer to this question, we could put fear to bed once and for all. While that seems like a nice thought, it's not likely. Fear is one of those things that many of us will constantly have to contend with. The problem, however, doesn't come in the contending, the problem arises because many of us fall victim to fear and refuse to fight. We surrender to it and allow it to govern us. There is no resolve, no struggle. We simply give in and allow it to run rampant in our lives. But why? Why do we allow fear to rob us of God's absolute best for our lives? To answer this question, we must first understand exactly what fear is.

Dictionary.com defines fear as an unpleasant emotion caused by the belief that someone or something is dangerous, likely to cause pain, or a threat. The Hebrew Bible makes mention of two types of fear, pachad and yirah. Pachad is a Hebrew word that means terror, dread, or great fear. Yirah is also a Hebrew word. It means awesome or terrifying thing, respect, reverence. It is the type of fear the Bible refers to when it says we are to fear God. I will expound on both of these later.

Examining Myself: Let's Look More Closely

Why am I so afraid? This is the question I kept asking myself as I sought to dismantle the thing that had held me bound for so long. What exactly was making me so fearful? Was it fear of success? Failure? Or some other elusive thing? Whatever it was, I decided it was time that I confronted it head on and questioned exactly why it had come.

Over the years I've had conversations with different people about the topic of fear, and I've typically gotten two types of responses. The first response is from the person who owns up to being afraid. This person acknowledges

Damn Fear

that fear has hindered them in some way, and is vulnerable enough to admit it. The second response is from the person who hasn't tapped in. They don't realize that the excuses they've given all these years for not pursuing their dream or that thing they are most passionate about are rooted in fear.

Fear has a way of masking itself as something else, and no where is this more obvious than in people's career and job choices. How many people have you met who are stuck in jobs they hate, yet they stay in them because it's convenient? They constantly complain, and get a nice paycheck every two weeks, but they are miserable. Why do people stay in dead end or even lucrative jobs for that matter, that they hate? Fear. They mask their staying with the need to make money, loyalty to other people, or comfort, they've gotten used to that place, those people, and don't want to have to start over somewhere else. Obviously, making money is important, but is it more important than your dreams? Let me rephrase that. Is it more important than your God-given dreams?

We've all heard the scripture, Mark 8:36, which says, "What does it profit a man to gain the whole world, but lose his soul?" Many of us look at this scripture and directly apply it to the person who has forfeited their soul for wealth and riches, but what if it could also apply to the person who forfeits the purpose and plans of God for the convenience and comfort of a bi-weekly paycheck? I'm not saying you should quit your job tomorrow. However, what I am saying is that you should be praying, seeking the face of God and strategizing on how you can use the place you are in, and what you currently have, to move you closer to your dreams and the thing God desires for you.

We all have seasons where we must do what we have to do to survive, but at some point, we should go from surviving to thriving. Thriving is what living void of the spirit of fear looks like. Oftentimes, the reasons we give ourselves for not pursuing something may be credible, but the truth is, if you've been telling yourself the same thing for years, then it's not your circumstances that are keeping you from living in purpose and destiny, it's fear. Your reasons are just a convenient excuse. *Ouch!*

***

Damn Fear

I remember being fresh out of college. I had just moved to Chicago and was having a hard time finding a job that would allow me to use my degree. I had graduated at the height of the recession, so finding any job during that time was a real challenge. Through the grace of God, I was able to land a job at Rainbow, a women's clothing store, the same company I had worked for while in college. Can I just say I hated that job? That's not what this part of the book is about, but I just thought I'd share that. LOL! Like, I literally hated it. I would go to work crying, be in the stock room crying, be on the work floor crying...LOL! It was rough! There were plenty of days I went in wishing they would fire me, because if I just quit, I'd never hear the end of it from my family. Anyway, let's get back to the main point. I worked at this store, and the thing I always found interesting was the number of people who worked there, and who had continued to work there for years, some for as many as ten or more, despite hating it.

Truthfully, these people were my motivation. I refused to get stuck like that, and this can easily happen when you encounter a series of disappointments. How many jobs did I apply for in that season, jobs that I was 100% qualified for, with no call backs or anything? Too many to recall. To say I was disappointed was an understatement. It took me about a year before I found another job, but other people I worked with had literally been there for years, and some without any real promotion or increase in pay. On the surface someone might say education, experience or skills kept them there, but that's not it. All three of those things are things we have control over. There are far too many programs available to assist people with these very things, for anyone to be stuck anywhere they don't want to be. I believe it was fear. Many of them had gotten comfortable and satisfied with where they were; and rather than rock the boat and go after what they really wanted, they settled for the convenience and comfort of the known.

As people we go through so many things that rob us of our ability to see beyond what's directly in front of us. It's easy to get distracted and jaded by circumstances. We desire more, but we allow the happenings in our life to dictate the moves we make, when we really should be making moves based upon our hopes and faith. In the end, we settle for the very things we despise because it's easy, and

Damn Fear

life is already hard. So why make it harder right? This is fear at work. It blurs our vision, and our ability to sift through what we really want; and is instigated by disillusion, disappointment, discouragement and dismay. All four of these feelings are drivers for the spirit of fear. Let's break them down.

Disillusion: disappointment resulting from the discovery that something is not as good as one believed it to be; to realize that a belief or an ideal is false

A good example of this would be some of the contestants we see on American Idol. You know the pre-show where they show you all the auditions. There's always that one person, who for whatever reason is under the illusion that they can sing. One note in, and we all know that is not so. They were truly deluded into believing they had the gift of singing, but the truth is someone should have told them, "Nah, that's not your gift." And it's ok that that isn't their gift, because we all have one, that's just not theirs. This is a funny example, but if you were to sit back and think about it you might discover some false illusions in your own life that led you to block your true purpose and dreams. In my own life, as I've pursued my dreams, I can see how I've fallen into disillusion.

At some point, after being in Chicago for a while, I got the vision to start Ashes for Beauty, a magazine for Black Christian women. When I first started the magazine, I actively looked for supporters and investors. I just knew the right person would come along and give me all the capital I needed to make my dream a reality. That never happened!

Along the way I met some people who gave me false hope, including some guy who claimed to work for Beyoncé's dad. I still don't know whether that was true or not, but that's another story for another day. After meeting with him late one night at a local restaurant, I never heard from him again, so I'm going to assume God was protecting me from whatever that was. There was also the meeting with the pastor's wife who after sharing my vision with her, told me I needed to get a clue. That was soul crushing. It took me a minute to bounce back from that one.

I don't mention any of these things to say that meeting someone who will instantly invest in

Damn Fear

you can never happen, and that God doesn't work in this way, but it is to say that my not receiving the support I so desperately needed and desired at that time, led to me being disappointed and discouraged, and that is where fear started to take root. We can't allow our expectations to throw us off track, or as I've learned from one of my friends, we need to learn how to manage our expectations. So many disappointments and let downs stem from mismanaged expectations.

I remember being so frustrated and angry with how things were going, that I just took my hands off of everything. But here's the gag. Feel your feelings, vent, get all of that out of the way, and then surrender your will, expectations, and illusions of how things should be to God. It's easy to be disappointed if we're more focused on how we think things should be, than on what God says is so.

Disappointment is another driver of fear.

Disappointment- defeated of expectation or hope; let down

Traneisha Y. Jones

Psychology Today defines disappointment as the uncomfortable space between our expectations and reality. There are a lot of us that can relate to this. You expect things to go a certain way, and you invest time, effort, money and other resources, and then nothing. Encounter enough of these instances, and it can literally knock the wind out of you. I've been there. The place where all of your efforts prove fruitless. More than anything else, I believe this is a big driver of fear. Some of us try, but then never try again because we don't want to be disappointed again, and others of us never try for fear of being disappointed the first time around.

I fall into the former category, but I know a lot of people in the latter. They don't hope or dream for much of anything, and they set their expectations super low, so that if something happens, they're not too disappointed at the outcome. Here's the thing, neither one is good, but I would rather try any day than not try at all. I believe we get what we hope for. God meets us at our point of expectation, so we might as well set them high.

Damn Fear

"The fears of the wicked will be fulfilled; the hopes of the godly will be granted."
— Proverbs 10:24 (NLT)

Let's break the word disappointment down further. Dis means without, and appointment refers to a specified day and time. I think we would do well to remember that God controls time, so even if we don't achieve something in one season, it doesn't mean it won't come back around.

The good news about disappointment is that there is still hope. So what it didn't work out! Try again. Aaliyah said it best, "If at first you don't succeed, dust yourself off and try again," but at no point, and in no way do you give up.

That's the challenging part, continuing to push and pursue when you've been met with disappointment after disappointment. But guess what? God is a restorer, and nothing is ever wasted. Every setback, every experience, every disappointment truly works together for our good. Just don't let it breed fear, instead take disappointment as a stepping stone to your next. Examine what you can do differently. Strategize. Think through the issue. If you allow disappointment to overtake you, soon weariness and indifference will follow, and you'll be too consumed by those things to hope or dream for anything.

Think about it this way. What's the alternative to settling into disappointment and allowing it to birth fear in your life and hinder you from pursuing your dreams? Which result are you okay with? Keep climbing.

"Being confident of this, that he who began a good work in you will carry it on to completion until the day of Christ Jesus."
– Philippians 1:6

Discouragement is another sign of fear at work. Let's define it and examine how it shows up.

Discouragement- having lost hope or confidence

Discouragement can come from experiences or from people. This is why I try not to discuss anything I'm planning or hoping to do with anyone until I'm assured of it myself, because one discouraging remark from someone else can literally knock you off your square and send

Damn Fear

you into fear mode. Sometimes people mean well and sometimes what they're saying is rooted in their own fear and insecurities. Whatever it is, you can't let what people say or don't say stop you from pursuing your dream. Oftentimes, we let what people say detract us from our goal, but sometimes it's also what they don't say.

We have this really great idea, but no one around us seems to understand or be in support of it. So what! You have to learn how to weigh things, and try the spirit by the Spirit. In other words, examine what they are saying. Sometimes what people are telling us is wisdom and we should take heed. Other times, the person can be a well-intentioned hater whose words or lack of support should have no bearing on what you do or don't do in pursuit of your dreams and goals. Seek God. Don't allow their negative outlook to jade your vision. Afterall, it's called YOUR vision for a reason.

Let's expound a little on support. No one has to support you, not even your mama. One of my all-time favorite quotes comes from the Blues Singer B.B. King, "Nobody loves me but my mama, and she could be jivin' too."

I know, ouch! Not my mama, lol! But it's the truth. Should they? Yes, because that's the purpose of family and friends. We should be there to support one another. But do they have to? No. And we would do well to count it lagniappe (a little something extra) when they do, that way if they don't, we won't be tempted to give up and throw in the towel because no one supports us. Are you doing what you're doing for support or for something else? Focus on the something else, the support will come, and even if it doesn't, it's still all good, and it's still all God.

"Have I not commanded you? Be strong and courageous. Do not be afraid; do not be discouraged, for the LORD your God will be with you wherever you go."
- Joshua 1:9

The last driver of fear is dismay.

Dismay- distress, typically caused by something unexpected; shock; worry

Have you ever worked yourself into a frenzy at the thought of pursuing something before you even set your hand to do it? The very thought

Damn Fear

of it worried and stressed you to the point that you did nothing at all. This is dismay. What about when you've finally started to pursue that dream or vision and then something happens- someone close passes away unexpectedly, a loved one becomes sick, your spouse loses their job, or your house burns down literally and figuratively? This is also dismay.

What unexpected thing stole your confidence and caused you to halt in the pursuit of your destiny? Go back and get it. Start again if you need to. Reset! Put your full weight on God; and remember your confidence should be in Him and what He's able to do.

"Fear thou not; for I am with thee; be not dismayed; for I am thy God: I will strengthen thee, yea, I will uphold thee with the right hand of my righteousness."
- Isaiah 41:10

"If you know the enemy and know yourself, you need not fear the results of a hundred battles."

— Sun Tzu

Chapter 2

Good Things Fall Apart

"Many of us crucify ourselves between two thieves, regret for the past, and fear of the future."

— Fulton Oursler

No one tells you that you can be really good at something and still fail, or that you can do everything you're "supposed" to do and still not see the results you desire. I had been an honor roll student all of my life. We were taught to study and go to class, and you would get good grades, get into a good college, graduate and then live the high life in a career that pays well. Though this sounds good for a young person seeking to position themselves for what our society calls the "good life," it doesn't take long after graduating from college and entering the real world to realize A+B does not always equal C, that there will be some variables tossed in from time to time, and that how you handle those things will ultimately send you down one path or another.

> **"First you make decisions,
> then your decisions make you."**
> **– Author unknown**

As a young woman in my early twenties, I'd never really faced any real disappointment, other than not going to Spelman College. I'd gotten accepted, but there was no way my family could afford the more than $20,000 a semester, and at that time Spelman didn't give scholarships to incoming freshman, so that was that.

Nothing quite prepared me for the disappointment and obstacles I would face when I decided to pursue my dreams. Honestly, even if someone had told me, I don't know if I would have believed them. I probably would have dismissed what they said as heresy. LBVS. The truth is some things can only be learned from first-hand experience. There's no level of anything anyone can tell you, you must go through it for yourself.

Damn Fear

I mentioned previously how I had gotten a job at Rainbow, and worked there briefly before landing another job, one that actually allowed me to use my degree. Well, that new job was short lived. I probably worked for that new company for about three months before they started laying people off en masse. I had no worries, for the most part everything was still good, or at least somewhat okay. Between unemployment and the financial support of my grandparents, I was able to keep my head above water.

Shortly before getting laid off, I had started Ashes for Beauty. I was doing most of the leg work, with the exception of a friend who helped me with the layout and design. I had also entered a small business competition at a local church hoping to win enough capital to help me launch everything I had envisioned. At this time, it had probably been about a year since I had been laid off. God had consistently provided, but then everything started drying up. By the time the competition wrapped up, I had managed to place fourth, but my prize was a marketing and branding package, no moolah. I was grateful, but what I had really been hoping for and needing did not come through.

Traneisha Y. Jones

On top of not winning the competition, my unemployment had dried up, and my family was no longer able to support me. It didn't take me long to realize it was time to move back home. All of this probably transpired on a Thursday or Friday, and by that following week I had packed up my car and was headed back to Louisiana.

In my heart I was sad, but I had a plan. I would stay home for a year, work and save, and then move back to Chicago to pursue my magazine. To make a long story short, I did just that. I got a job as the Communications Specialist for a community program at Southern University and A & M College. I worked there for roughly a year before heading back to Chicago. I wish I could say that when I returned everything was all good, but it wasn't. It was actually worse. I lived with family briefly, and when that didn't work out, I moved into a hotel. I don't even remember how long I did that, but it was for a nice while. During this time, I worked retail jobs, and eventually I started freelancing which led to me starting my own media and communications company, T. Jones Media.

Oh yeah, I can't leave this out. As I mentioned before, I had moved back to Chicago to pursue

Damn Fear

my magazine. So the entire time I'm going through transitions with work and my living arrangements, I'm also working on the magazine. My first celebrity cover story interview was with actress Tasha Smith, known mostly for her role as Angela in Tyler Perry's *Why Did I Get Married?*, and was conducted via the phone in the bathroom of my job. It was the only place I could find absolute quiet, and my manager at the time was nice enough to let me do it. With the little money I had, I hired someone to do marketing for the launch party I was planning to have for the magazine. The person I hired did absolutely nothing. I mean zip, nada... they yielded zero results. Anything they did do was things I had already done for myself. LBVS. This is actually how the marketing arm of my business was birthed. Remember I told you, *God wastes nothing.*

I had gotten all these wonderful writers, gotten a designer to lay out the magazine, hired a marketer, secured a celebrity interview, solicited businesses for ads and sponsorships, and even secured some, and still nothing. I can't say there was no fruit, it just wasn't the fruit I was looking for. I was back to square one, and to top it all off I had exhausted all of my energy, time, money and resources, only to produce nothing. I was so frustrated, but God was still good. Though everything had failed with the magazine, my media and communications business had started to pick up. Honestly, I wasn't even trying to pursue this, it just kind of happened. God truly orders our steps, and that's my message to you. There's a quote that says, "Good things fall apart, so that better things can fall together." I believe this wholeheartedly. We have no control over how things will turn out, our only task is to pursue, have faith and take decisive action, the rest is literally up to God.

Unfortunately, this is where many of us get stuck. I know I did, and it took me a while to get unstuck. I literally put everything related to the magazine in a box and vowed never to touch it again. I was just that frustrated! How could God give me a vision and not help bring it to pass? Didn't He see my struggle? Didn't He understand my pain? Didn't He see my disappointment? Yes, yes, and yes, and guess what, it was still working together for my good. God has not forgotten. The vision is for an appointed time. Keep the faith and don't allow your heart to be consumed by fear.

Damn Fear

I want to say that God is always out to prove something, but I think the better thing to say is that God is always out to prune something.

"The purpose of pruning is to improve the quality of the roses, not to hurt the bush."
-Florence Littauer

God doesn't have to prove anything. We, however, do need pruning that will allow us to truly be a reflection of Him and who He has called us to be. So, what needs to be pruned? Fear- fear of the future, fear of uncertainty, fear of lack, fear of making a mistake, fear of being successful, fear of repeating patterns, and so on. We need to replace fear with faith and trust that even if things don't work out as we planned or envisioned, God is more than able to do what He said He would do. And what does He say He will do? Seek Him and find out.

"We were meant to live for so much more, have we lost ourselves."

— *Switchfoot*

Chapter 3
The Convenience of Settling

"The enemy uses fear to decrease our hope, and limit our victories."
— Jessica Kastner

I've been waiting to get to this chapter, because this is where fear leaves most of us. We end up settling into mediocrity because it's comfortable, convenient and there is no real conflict, except the conflict we have with ourselves of course. From day to day, it may not hit you, but you can't tell me that when you get to a quiet space, and you're truly thinking and reflecting on your life, that you don't also realize that you've settled in one area or another. No one has to tell you this either. Some of us settle for jobs because it's convenient, others of us settle for relationships because we're afraid of being alone. Still others settle for places because they're too afraid to break out and go somewhere different. *Dang!* Fear is riding your back the entire time, and you're letting it. It's got you settling in places where you should be thriving!

Let's look at the story of Esau and Jacob found in Genesis 25. Most of us know the story. Esau is famished, he comes in from hunting, and Jacob manages to trick him out of his birthright in exchange for a meal. So, what does this have to do with us and this whole idea of settling for mediocrity?

Let's look more closely at Esau. Though they were twins, Esau was the first-born son, so he was entitled to receive the birthright, which was centered around position and inheritance. Esau was famished, even though he was doing something he was skilled at, and in a moment that was truly temporary, he forfeits his birthright for temporary gain. He literally exchanges his inheritance and what was rightly his for a hot meal. How many of us do this? We get caught up in the temporary frill of circumstances and forfeit everything God has for us because we can't see beyond that moment. We devalue the gift. We devalue the calling; and we don't consider the significance of our dreams. Like Esau, we get caught up in surviving, so who cares about tomorrow, when

Damn Fear

I don't even know if I'm going to make it through today. We have the mentality of surviving versus thriving, and we literally despise the very thing meant to prosper us and align us with God's will for our lives.

I met a girl recently who talked about how she had been so busy surviving, she never even considered what she really wanted to do with her life. "A dream? What's that?" She shared how she had been in the foster care system, and had gotten married and had children at a young age. She was in her late twenties now, and had spent so many years caring for her family, and just trying to make it from one day to the next, that she never had the chance to stop to catch her breath, and truly think about what it is that she wanted out of life.

There are so many people like this. They're so locked into the daily grind of life, that they literally never have a moment to reset or reconsider exactly what they want out of it or what God wants for them for that matter. They desire more, but they don't even know what it looks like to hope for that. They don't have the *dollar or the dream*. They are merely existing!

So how do we break free from this, and learn to thrive instead of simply surviving. We'll explore this in the next chapter.

"You have the power to revoke [fear] at any moment."

— Marcus Aurelius

Chapter 4
Stir Up the Gift

"God has not given us the Spirit of fear, but what the Lord has given us... power."
– Joe Pace & the Colorado Mass Choir

To go from surviving to thriving, we must stir up the gift that God has placed inside of us.

"Therefore I remind you to stir up the gift of God which is in you through the laying on of my hands. For God has not given us a spirit of fear, but of power and of love and of a sound mind."   – 2 Timothy 1:6-7

According to commentary, stir up the gift in this context means to rekindle or resuscitate, cultivate, to use. In other words, we need to use the gifts God has put in us. I won't go too in depth with this, because I believe the scripture speaks for itself, but in essence it says God has not given us the spirit of fear, but of power and of love and of a sound mind. So no fear, but power. Power in this scripture refers to dynamis, force (literal or figurative), miraculous power, ability, abundance, might, strength. What are you afraid of again? Remember, God has given you power to overcome any obstacle.

The second thing God gives us instead of fear is love. As the scripture says in 1 John 4:18, "There is no fear in love; but perfect love casteth out fear: because fear hath torment. He that feareth is not made perfect in love."

Lastly, He gives us a sound mind, which means discipline, self-control. It also means He gives us peace of mind, so that we don't have to be bogged down with worry and dread, and all the other things that attempt to keep us in fear.

Mike Walsh, pastor of a local church in Wyoming had this to say about the sound mind God gives us, "This phrase, "sound mind," is taken from the Greek word sophroneo, which is a compound word combining sodzo and phroneo. The Greek word sodzo means to be saved or delivered. It suggests something that is delivered, rescued, revived, salvaged, and protected and is now safe and secure. The

Traneisha Y. Jones

second part of the phrase "sound mind" comes from the Greek word phroneo, which carries the idea of a person's intelligence or total frame of thinking- including his rationale, logic, and emotions. When the words sodzo and phroneo are compounded into one word, they form the word sophroneo, which pictures a mind that has been delivered, rescued, revived, and salvaged."*

In other words, you don't have to give in to the spirit of fear, God has more than equipped us with everything we need to overcome and resist the lies the enemy tries to overtake our mind with.

---

*Mike Walsh, "God has given us a sound mind," *Powell Tribune*, June 4, 2020, https://www.powelltribune.com/stories/god-has-given-us-a-sound-mind,25654

"When you give voice to your fear, when you expose it, as vulnerable as that makes you, you give others the same permission. You give them courage to believe there's more to life than cowering. You give hope. And my guess is, when you tackle your inner fears, you will eventually tackle what's held you back from who God intended you to be. Your fears lead you to who you really are."

-Chris Fabry

Chapter 5

The Voices of Fear

"Our doubts are traitors and make us lose the good we often might win, by fearing to attempt."
— Jane Addams

To overcome the spirit of fear, it is important to identify the voices of fear that may arise. Each of these things are a sign of fear at work in your life. They include:

- Self-doubt
- Procrastination
- Indecisiveness
- Perfectionism
- Caring too much about what others think
- Skewed perspective

However they show up, we can counter them with the Word of God, and overcome any mind-traps they attempt to set.

Damn Fear

Self-doubt

Self-doubt is a big one, but only because often when it shows up, it also means that we have taken our focus off of God and placed it on ourselves. How much of our destiny has been forfeited because of self-doubt? We literally talk ourselves out of our dreams because we don't think we're good enough, or we think we're too much of this, or not enough of that. We're too old, we're too young. We're too uneducated, or we don't have enough experience. None of this is true and has any bearing on the pursuit of your dreams and goals, but for the sake of entertaining you and your doubts, let's just pretend that it is. Let's pretend that everything you tell yourself about who you are and what you are not is true. What then? What does that really mean? Does it mean that you can't go after your dream or that thing you are most passionate about? Probably not. Make a plan and get to work.

When self-doubt rises, cling to Philippians 4:13 which says, "I can do all things through Christ who strengthens me."

Procrastination is another sign of fear at work in our life. I've literally struggled with this one since I was young, but it can be overcome.

Procrastination

One wise man said, "Action will destroy your procrastination." Want to counter it with the Word? Try Proverbs 6:4, "Don't put it off; do it now! Don't rest until you do." Like Nike, just do it!

Indecisiveness

Personally, indecisiveness annoys me. Most people who exhibit this know exactly what they want to do, they have an unction of what they should do, yet they do nothing because they're afraid they'll make the wrong decision. Here's the thing. Deciding to do nothing, or going in circles regarding a decision, is a decision too. The question is, is it yielding the fruit you want? If not, it's best you choose differently.

James 1:8 says, "A double-minded man is unstable in all his ways." To overcome indecisiveness just make a decision! I know it sounds simple, but failing to do this will literally have you going in the same circles. A helpful tool, use former U.S. Secretary of State Colin Powell's 40/70 rule which says you should have no less than 40%, and no more than 70% of the information you need to make a tough decision. If you have less than 40% of information before making a decision, you may choose wrong, and waiting for 100% of the information before making a decision may prove to be too late. We can only make decisions based on what we have or know in the moment, everything else is guess work.

Perfectionism

Aye ya ya, this is a big one too. Waiting until things are perfect will have you doing just that, waiting. While aiming for perfection can sometimes be a good thing, being consumed by the idea of being 100% perfect can also prove to be faulty. Sometimes you have to learn to let go, especially if it means being stagnant or not moving forward with your dream or goal. As Winston Churchill once said, "Perfection is the enemy of completion."

Traneisha Y. Jones

Opinion of Others

David Icke wrote, "The greatest prison people live in is the fear of what other people think." The opinions of others can definitely thwart our efforts to pursue our dreams. So how do we block this and proceed forward? As Proverbs 29:25 says, "It is dangerous to be concerned with what others think of you, but if you trust the Lord, you are safe." Want to block out the opinions of others? Trust what God says over the opinions of man.

Skewed Perspective

A skewed perspective can have us making a mountain out of a mole hill, and grossly exaggerating something that's really not that big of a deal. Consider the story of Peter. Peter literally asks Jesus to call him out on to the water, and just as Jesus does, he takes a few steps before he begins to sink. It wasn't that Jesus couldn't keep him from sinking. Peter sank because he took his eyes off of Christ, and placed them on the circumstances around him. A skewed perspective will have you forgetting the very thing you prayed to God for. If He

Damn Fear

called you to it, He'll bring you through it. No need to sink or be consumed by fear, keep your eyes and attention on Him and the task at hand.

"Each of us must confront our own fears, must come face to face with them. How we handle our fears will determine where we go with the rest of our lives. To experience adventure or to be limited by the fear of it."

— Judy Blume

Chapter 6

Name Your Fear

> "Fear is nothing more than a state of mind."
> — Napoleon Hill

At any moment any of us can fall victim to fear, even in those moments when we should be excited and overjoyed. Jewish Rabbi Alan Lew taught that the Hebrew Bible uses two words for fear pachad and yirah.

Pachad

Pachad is the fear that most of us are familiar with. It is irrational. Psychologist Dr. Karl Albrecht describes it as fear that "freezes us, paralyzes us and that prevents us from actualizing our full potential." It is the fear that consumes us when are worried about what could happen or our minds have imagined the worse-case scenario.

Traneisha Y. Jones

Yirah

Rabbi Alan Lew defined Yirah as "the fear that overcomes us when we suddenly find ourselves in possession of considerably more energy than we are used to, inhabiting a larger space than we are used to inhabiting, and the feeling we get when we are in the presence of something sacred or divine." This is the kind of fear we encounter when we're stepping out to do something new.

Understanding the difference between these two types of fear can help us to not only identify the fear at work in our life, but also overcome it, so that it does not stagnate us. I once read a book where the author shared an exercise called Seven Levels Deep. Doing this exercise can help you get to the core of exactly what you are afraid of, so that you can break free and not allow the fear to hinder you from progressing forward.

Here's what you should do. First ask yourself what you are afraid of. Next ask yourself why. Keep asking yourself why in response to each answer you give, up to seven times, until you get to the root. Once you have narrowed down

Damn Fear

your why, find a scripture that counters it. For example, if your reason is fear of failure, you can counter it with Psalm 73:26, "My flesh and my heart may fail, but God is the strength of my heart and my portion forever."

While pachad is the fear that most of us are familiar with, I think it's important to really look at yirah as well. In my own life, when things are going well, God is opening doors, and new things are happening, I have felt yirah at work. It's that feeling of bigness. Truthfully, it can be debilitating as well. You can be so used to things going wrong, that when things go right, you feel overwhelmed and anxious, so if we're not careful, yirah can also cause us to retreat from what we should be embracing and celebrating.

Yirah is also the fear we feel when we are in the presence of God. It is awe and reverence. I have felt this fear as well, and is one that we should strive to consistently embrace and be consumed by. As Psalm 16:11 says, "In the presence of God, there is fullness of joy."

"The cave you fear to enter holds the treasure you seek."

— *Napoleon Hill*

Chapter 7
Defeating the Giant of Fear

"And Moses said to the people, "Do not be afraid. Stand still, and see the salvation of the LORD, which He will accomplish for you today. For the Egyptians whom you see today, you shall again no more forever. The LORD will fight for you, and you shall hold your peace." And the Lord said to Moses, "Why do you cry to Me? Tell the children of Israel to go forward."   – Exodus 14:13-15

Now that we have identified the root of fear and how it shows up in our life, how do we defeat it? As one wise man once said, "Feel the fear and do it anyway." In other words, the best way to overcome fear is to take action.

> "Inaction breeds doubt and fear."
> -Dale Carnegie

Traneisha Y. Jones

In addition to taking decisive action, to conquer fear we must also learn to control our imagination and thought process.

As Philippians 4:8 says, "Finally, brethren, whatsoever things are true, whatsoever things are honest, whatsoever things are just, whatsoever things are pure, whatsoever things are lovely, whatsoever things are of good report, if there be any virtue and if there be any praise, think on these things."

If fear is nothing more than a state of mind, then we know the battle for our dreams and goals also starts in the mind. We would do well to keep ourselves rooted in faith and possibilities. If God is for us, then who can be against us? Repeat that until you get it, "If God is for me, then who can be against me."

Faith in God and His abilities, and the abilities He's given us, along with power, love and a sound mind thwart anything we could ever be afraid of. In the shadow of God these things are minute and of null effect. So, we may feel afraid, but before fear can consume us we must take care to settle ourselves in the Word of God and reset our hearts and minds.

Damn Fear

We must do like David when he encountered Goliath... face everything and rise. Who or what is this fear to knock me off of my square and out of the promises of God?!

You've got this! It's time to bury the what ifs, self-doubt, and any illusions you've bought into. Determine that fear will no longer hold you hostage or keep you from moving forward.

Mark 5:36, "But Jesus refused to listen to what they were told and said to the Jewish official, "Don't yield to fear. All you need to do is to keep on believing."

#DamnFear

"God has not given us the spirit of fear, but of POWER and of LOVE, and of a SOUND MIND."

-2 Timothy 1:7

Traneisha Y. Jones

Scriptures for Overcoming Fear

John 16:33, "I have told you these things, so that in me you may have peace. In this world you will have trouble. But take heart! I have overcome the world."

Isaiah 41:13, "For I, the LORD your God, hold your right hand; it is I who say to you, 'Fear not, I am the one who helps you.'"

1 John 4:18, "There is no fear in love, but perfect love casts out fear. For fear has to do with punishment, and whoever fears has not been perfected in love."

Joshua 1:9, "Have not I commanded thee? Be strong and of good courage; be not afraid, neither be thou dismayed: for the LORD thy God is with thee whithersoever thou goest."

Psalm 23:4, "Even though I walk through the valley of the shadow of death, I will fear no evil, for you are with me; your rod and your staff, they comfort me."

Damn Fear

Psalm 27:1, "The Lord is my light and my salvation; whom shall I fear? The Lord is the stronghold of my life; of whom shall I be afraid?"

Luke 12:7, "Indeed, the very hairs of your head are all numbered. Don't be afraid; you are worth more than many sparrows."

Isaiah 35:4, "Say to those who have an anxious heart, 'Be strong; fear not! Behold, your God will come with vengeance, with the recompense of God. He will come and save you.'"

Psalm 46:1-3, "God is our refuge and strength, a very present help in trouble. Therefore we will not fear though the earth gives way, though the mountains be moved in the heart of the sea, though its waters roar and foam, though the mountains tremble at its swelling."

Deuteronomy 3:22, "You shall not fear them, for it is the LORD your God who fights for you."

Afterword

"Oh my soul you are not alone. There's a place where fear has to face the God you know." – Casting Crowns

Welcome to the other side of fear! The side where you're thriving and unencumbered by fear. The side where your dreams blossom. Life is not without obstacles, but you've learned how to navigate them, and not allow fear to stagnate you in the process.

I'm believing God will use the very words of this book to transform your life from the inside-out. I pray He will do a radical work in you, and that any area of your life fear has attempted to keep you bound in will be no more. Oftentimes, before the Word has had the opportunity to firmly take root, the enemy comes in to do "transformation control." But not so! We cast off the restraints of fear, and trust that God will empower you to walk in the freedom that comes from surrendering and fully trusting in Him.

Damn Fear

I pray that the words of this book will germinate and produce fruit in your life, and that you will immediately see the effects of what happens when you cast off fear and fully lean into the truth of God's Word! I'm excited for you. Excited for your destiny! Excited for your now! You are no longer a slave to fear.

Prayer

Dear Abba,

You said in your Word that these You hold in your hand, You will in no way pluck out. I know that my life and times are in your hands, so I trust your perfect will for my life. I also trust You to bind the spirit of fear, and thank You for giving me power, love and a sound mind. Help me Lord to be as bold as a lion, assured of your Word and calling on my life.

Cast down every thought and imagination that exalts itself against You and your Word. Help me to operate in truth. Help me to cling to that, and remind me of your truth in moments I feel doubtful and uncertain. Order my steps. Help me to be the person You have called me to be. Please don't allow fear to sabotage my life or

Traneisha Y. Jones

hinder me from being everything You have called me to be. I surrender myself to You, and I trust that anything that comes my way, You will help me to overcome. In Jesus name I pray, Amen.

Questions for Reflection

What dreams or goals do you have?
_____
_____
_____
_____
_____

Has fear prevented you from pursuing any of those dreams or goals?
_____
_____
_____
_____
_____

What are you afraid of?
_____
_____
_____
_____
_____

Why are you afraid?

_____
_____
_____
_____
_____

What steps can you take to overcome fear in your life?

_____
_____
_____
_____
_____

Revisit the Scriptures for Overcoming Fear or make a list of additional scriptures you can reflect on whenever fear tries to overtake you.

_____
_____
_____
_____
_____

Recommended Reading

The Dream Giver
by Bruce Wilkinson

How to Bloom Where You Are Planted
by Dearal L. Jordan

About the Author

Dr. Traneisha Jones is a faith and lifestyle writer, speaker and serial entrepreneur who passionately fosters the growth and development of leaders across the globe. As an international business strategist and publishing consultant, she has helped hundreds of leaders leverage their gifts and voice in the marketplace. Connect with her on IG @tjonesmedia or at www.tjonesmedia.com.

www.ingramcontent.com/pod-product-compliance
Lightning Source LLC
Chambersburg PA
CBHW052120110526
44592CB00013B/1691